50 Premium Cake Recipes

By: Kelly Johnson

Table of Contents

- Classic Red Velvet Cake
- Tiramisu Cake
- Chocolate Fudge Cake
- Lemon Blueberry Cake
- Carrot Cake with Cream Cheese Frosting
- Almond Flourless Cake
- Salted Caramel Chocolate Cake
- Coconut Cream Cake
- Raspberry Swirl Cheesecake
- Espresso Mocha Cake
- Strawberry Shortcake
- Black Forest Cake
- Churro Cake
- Chocolate Hazelnut Cake
- Funfetti Cake
- Lemon Poppy Seed Cake
- Pineapple Upside-Down Cake
- Pistachio Rose Cake
- Orange and Almond Cake
- White Chocolate Raspberry Cake
- Cherry Almond Cake
- Hummingbird Cake
- Peach Cobbler Cake
- Peanut Butter Chocolate Cake
- Tres Leches Cake
- Poppy Seed Cake
- Caramelized Banana Cake
- German Chocolate Cake
- Mocha Hazelnut Cake
- Vanilla Bean Pound Cake
- Coconut Pineapple Cake
- Pumpkin Spice Cake
- Black Sesame Cake
- Chocolate Mousse Cake
- Matcha Green Tea Cake

- S'mores Cake
- Maple Pecan Cake
- Lime Coconut Cake
- Vanilla Chiffon Cake
- Brown Sugar Cinnamon Cake
- Apricot Almond Cake
- Spiced Apple Cake
- Meringue Layer Cake
- Baked Alaska Cake
- Lemon Raspberry Meringue Cake
- Key Lime Cake
- Lavender Honey Cake
- Chococherry Cake
- Apple Cinnamon Streusel Cake
- White Chocolate Mint Cake

Classic Red Velvet Cake

Ingredients:

- 2 1/2 cups all-purpose flour
- 1 1/2 cups granulated sugar
- 1 teaspoon baking soda
- 1 teaspoon cocoa powder
- 1/2 teaspoon salt
- 1 1/2 cups vegetable oil
- 1 cup buttermilk
- 2 large eggs
- 2 tablespoons red food coloring
- 1 teaspoon vanilla extract
- 1 teaspoon white vinegar

For Cream Cheese Frosting:

- 1 package (8 oz) cream cheese, softened
- 1/4 cup unsalted butter, softened
- 4 cups powdered sugar
- 1 teaspoon vanilla extract

Instructions:

1. Preheat the oven to 350°F (175°C). Grease and flour two 9-inch round cake pans.
2. In a bowl, mix the flour, sugar, baking soda, cocoa powder, and salt.
3. In another bowl, whisk together the oil, buttermilk, eggs, food coloring, vanilla extract, and vinegar.
4. Add the wet ingredients to the dry ingredients and mix until smooth.
5. Divide the batter evenly between the two cake pans and bake for 30-35 minutes or until a toothpick comes out clean.
6. Cool the cakes in the pans for 10 minutes, then transfer to a wire rack to cool completely.
7. For the frosting, beat together the cream cheese, butter, powdered sugar, and vanilla until smooth.
8. Frost the cooled cakes with cream cheese frosting and serve.

Tiramisu Cake

Ingredients:

- 1 box of vanilla cake mix
- 1 cup brewed espresso, cooled
- 1/2 cup coffee liqueur (optional)
- 1 1/2 cups mascarpone cheese
- 1 1/2 cups heavy whipping cream
- 1/4 cup powdered sugar
- 1 teaspoon vanilla extract
- Unsweetened cocoa powder for dusting

Instructions:

1. Prepare the vanilla cake mix according to the package directions, then allow the cakes to cool completely.
2. Mix the espresso and coffee liqueur together in a bowl. Brush the cakes with the coffee mixture.
3. In a large bowl, whisk mascarpone, heavy cream, powdered sugar, and vanilla until stiff peaks form.
4. Place one layer of cake on a serving platter, spread a layer of the mascarpone mixture, and top with the second cake layer.
5. Frost the top with the remaining mascarpone mixture and dust with cocoa powder.
6. Chill for a few hours before serving.

Chocolate Fudge Cake

Ingredients:

- 1 3/4 cups all-purpose flour
- 1 1/2 cups granulated sugar
- 3/4 cup cocoa powder
- 1 1/2 teaspoons baking powder
- 1 1/2 teaspoons baking soda
- 1/2 teaspoon salt
- 2 eggs
- 1 cup milk
- 1/2 cup vegetable oil
- 2 teaspoons vanilla extract
- 1 cup boiling water

For Fudge Frosting:

- 1/2 cup butter, softened
- 1/4 cup cocoa powder
- 2 cups powdered sugar
- 1/4 cup milk
- 1 teaspoon vanilla extract

Instructions:

1. Preheat the oven to 350°F (175°C). Grease and flour two 9-inch round cake pans.
2. In a large bowl, mix the flour, sugar, cocoa powder, baking powder, baking soda, and salt.
3. Add the eggs, milk, oil, and vanilla. Mix until smooth. Stir in the boiling water (the batter will be thin).
4. Pour the batter into the prepared cake pans and bake for 30-35 minutes.
5. For the frosting, combine butter, cocoa powder, powdered sugar, milk, and vanilla in a saucepan over medium heat. Stir until smooth.
6. Frost the cooled cakes with the fudge frosting and serve.

Lemon Blueberry Cake

Ingredients:

- 2 cups all-purpose flour
- 1 1/2 cups granulated sugar
- 1 teaspoon baking powder
- 1/2 teaspoon baking soda
- 1/2 teaspoon salt
- 1/2 cup unsalted butter, softened
- 2 large eggs
- 1 cup buttermilk
- Zest of 1 lemon
- 1 cup fresh blueberries

For Lemon Frosting:

- 1/2 cup unsalted butter, softened
- 3 cups powdered sugar
- 2 tablespoons fresh lemon juice
- 1 tablespoon lemon zest
- 2-3 tablespoons milk

Instructions:

1. Preheat the oven to 350°F (175°C). Grease and flour two 9-inch round cake pans.
2. In a bowl, mix the flour, sugar, baking powder, baking soda, and salt.
3. In another bowl, beat together the butter and eggs until smooth, then add the buttermilk and lemon zest.
4. Gradually add the dry ingredients to the wet ingredients, stirring until smooth. Gently fold in the blueberries.
5. Pour the batter into the prepared pans and bake for 25-30 minutes or until a toothpick comes out clean.
6. For the frosting, beat together the butter, powdered sugar, lemon juice, and lemon zest until smooth. Add milk to reach your desired consistency.
7. Frost the cooled cakes with lemon frosting and serve.

Carrot Cake with Cream Cheese Frosting

Ingredients:

- 2 cups all-purpose flour
- 2 teaspoons baking powder
- 1 teaspoon baking soda
- 1 teaspoon cinnamon
- 1/2 teaspoon salt
- 4 large eggs
- 1 1/2 cups granulated sugar
- 1/2 cup vegetable oil
- 2 teaspoons vanilla extract
- 3 cups grated carrots
- 1/2 cup chopped walnuts (optional)

For Cream Cheese Frosting:

- 1 package (8 oz) cream cheese, softened
- 1/2 cup unsalted butter, softened
- 4 cups powdered sugar
- 1 teaspoon vanilla extract

Instructions:

1. Preheat the oven to 350°F (175°C). Grease and flour two 9-inch round cake pans.
2. In a bowl, combine the flour, baking powder, baking soda, cinnamon, and salt.
3. In another bowl, beat the eggs, sugar, oil, and vanilla until smooth. Gradually add the dry ingredients, then fold in the grated carrots and walnuts.
4. Pour the batter into the prepared pans and bake for 30-35 minutes.
5. For the frosting, beat the cream cheese, butter, powdered sugar, and vanilla until smooth.
6. Frost the cooled cakes with cream cheese frosting and serve.

Almond Flourless Cake

Ingredients:

- 1 1/2 cups almond flour
- 1/2 cup granulated sugar
- 1/4 cup unsweetened cocoa powder
- 1/4 teaspoon salt
- 4 large eggs
- 1 teaspoon vanilla extract
- 1/2 cup unsalted butter, melted
- Powdered sugar for dusting

Instructions:

1. Preheat the oven to 350°F (175°C). Grease and line a 9-inch round cake pan.
2. In a bowl, mix almond flour, sugar, cocoa powder, and salt.
3. In another bowl, whisk the eggs, vanilla extract, and melted butter. Combine with the dry ingredients and mix until smooth.
4. Pour the batter into the cake pan and bake for 25-30 minutes or until a toothpick comes out clean.
5. Cool completely, dust with powdered sugar, and serve.

Salted Caramel Chocolate Cake

Ingredients:

- 1 1/2 cups all-purpose flour
- 1 1/2 cups granulated sugar
- 1/2 cup unsweetened cocoa powder
- 1 teaspoon baking soda
- 1/2 teaspoon baking powder
- 1/2 teaspoon salt
- 2 large eggs
- 1 cup buttermilk
- 1/2 cup vegetable oil
- 2 teaspoons vanilla extract

For Salted Caramel Sauce:

- 1 cup granulated sugar
- 6 tablespoons unsalted butter
- 1/2 cup heavy cream
- 1 teaspoon sea salt

Instructions:

1. Preheat the oven to 350°F (175°C). Grease and flour two 9-inch round cake pans.
2. In a bowl, mix flour, sugar, cocoa powder, baking soda, baking powder, and salt.
3. In another bowl, whisk together eggs, buttermilk, oil, and vanilla. Gradually add the dry ingredients and mix until smooth.
4. Pour the batter into the prepared pans and bake for 30-35 minutes.
5. For the salted caramel sauce, heat the sugar in a saucepan over medium heat until it melts. Add butter, cream, and sea salt, and stir until smooth.
6. Frost the cooled cakes with salted caramel sauce and serve.

Coconut Cream Cake

Ingredients:

- 2 cups all-purpose flour
- 1 1/2 teaspoons baking powder
- 1/2 teaspoon baking soda
- 1/4 teaspoon salt
- 1/2 cup unsalted butter, softened
- 1 cup granulated sugar
- 2 large eggs
- 1 cup coconut milk
- 1 teaspoon vanilla extract
- 1/2 cup shredded coconut

For Coconut Frosting:

- 1 package (8 oz) cream cheese, softened
- 1/2 cup unsalted butter, softened
- 4 cups powdered sugar
- 1 teaspoon vanilla extract
- 1/2 cup shredded coconut

Instructions:

1. Preheat the oven to 350°F (175°C). Grease and flour two 9-inch round cake pans.
2. Mix flour, baking powder, baking soda, and salt in a bowl.
3. Beat together the butter and sugar in another bowl until creamy. Add eggs, coconut milk, and vanilla extract, and mix until smooth.
4. Gradually add the dry ingredients and fold in shredded coconut.
5. Pour the batter into the prepared pans and bake for 25-30 minutes.
6. For the frosting, beat cream cheese, butter, powdered sugar, vanilla extract, and coconut until smooth.
7. Frost the cooled cakes with coconut frosting and serve.

Raspberry Swirl Cheesecake

Ingredients:

- 1 1/2 cups graham cracker crumbs
- 1/4 cup sugar
- 1/2 cup unsalted butter, melted
- 4 packages (8 oz each) cream cheese, softened
- 1 1/2 cups granulated sugar
- 3 large eggs
- 1 teaspoon vanilla extract
- 1/4 cup sour cream
- 1/2 cup raspberry puree (fresh or frozen raspberries blended)

Instructions:

1. Preheat the oven to 325°F (160°C). Grease a 9-inch springform pan.
2. Mix graham cracker crumbs, sugar, and melted butter. Press into the bottom of the pan and bake for 10 minutes.
3. Beat cream cheese, sugar, eggs, vanilla extract, and sour cream until smooth. Pour half of the mixture into the pan.
4. Drop spoonfuls of raspberry puree over the cheesecake batter and swirl with a knife.
5. Bake for 50-60 minutes. Cool, then chill in the fridge for at least 4 hours before serving.

Espresso Mocha Cake

Ingredients:

- 1 3/4 cups all-purpose flour
- 1 1/2 cups granulated sugar
- 3/4 cup unsweetened cocoa powder
- 1 1/2 teaspoons baking powder
- 1 teaspoon baking soda
- 1/2 teaspoon salt
- 2 large eggs
- 1 cup brewed espresso, cooled
- 1/2 cup milk
- 1/2 cup vegetable oil
- 2 teaspoons vanilla extract
- 1/2 cup sour cream

For Mocha Frosting:

- 1/2 cup unsalted butter, softened
- 1/4 cup unsweetened cocoa powder
- 2 cups powdered sugar
- 1 tablespoon brewed espresso
- 1 teaspoon vanilla extract

Instructions:

1. Preheat the oven to 350°F (175°C). Grease and flour two 9-inch round cake pans.
2. In a bowl, mix the flour, sugar, cocoa powder, baking powder, baking soda, and salt.
3. In another bowl, whisk together the eggs, espresso, milk, oil, vanilla, and sour cream.
4. Gradually add the wet ingredients to the dry ingredients, mixing until smooth.
5. Divide the batter evenly between the prepared pans and bake for 30-35 minutes.
6. For the frosting, beat together the butter, cocoa powder, powdered sugar, espresso, and vanilla until smooth.
7. Frost the cooled cakes with mocha frosting and serve.

Strawberry Shortcake

Ingredients:

- 2 cups all-purpose flour
- 1/4 cup granulated sugar
- 1 tablespoon baking powder
- 1/2 teaspoon salt
- 1/2 cup unsalted butter, chilled and cubed
- 2/3 cup heavy cream, plus more for brushing
- 1 teaspoon vanilla extract
- 1 1/2 cups fresh strawberries, sliced
- 1/4 cup granulated sugar (for strawberries)
- Whipped cream for serving

Instructions:

1. Preheat the oven to 400°F (200°C). Grease and flour a baking sheet.
2. In a bowl, mix the flour, sugar, baking powder, and salt.
3. Cut the butter into the dry ingredients until it resembles coarse crumbs.
4. Add the heavy cream and vanilla extract, mixing until combined.
5. Turn the dough onto a floured surface and gently knead a few times. Roll out to 1-inch thickness and cut into rounds.
6. Place the rounds on the baking sheet, brush with cream, and bake for 12-15 minutes.
7. Toss the sliced strawberries with sugar and let them sit for 10 minutes to release juices.
8. To assemble, split the shortcake rounds in half, add a layer of strawberries and whipped cream, then top with the other half of the shortcake.

Black Forest Cake

Ingredients:

- 2 cups all-purpose flour
- 2 cups granulated sugar
- 3/4 cup unsweetened cocoa powder
- 1 1/2 teaspoons baking powder
- 1 1/2 teaspoons baking soda
- 1 teaspoon salt
- 3 large eggs
- 1 cup buttermilk
- 1/2 cup vegetable oil
- 2 teaspoons vanilla extract
- 1 cup hot water
- 1 jar (16 oz) dark cherry preserves or pie filling
- 2 cups heavy whipping cream
- 2 tablespoons powdered sugar
- Chocolate shavings for garnish

Instructions:

1. Preheat the oven to 350°F (175°C). Grease and flour two 9-inch round cake pans.
2. In a large bowl, combine the flour, sugar, cocoa powder, baking powder, baking soda, and salt.
3. In another bowl, whisk together the eggs, buttermilk, oil, and vanilla. Add the wet ingredients to the dry ingredients and mix until smooth.
4. Gradually add the hot water and mix until combined (batter will be thin).
5. Pour the batter evenly into the cake pans and bake for 30-35 minutes.
6. Whip the cream and powdered sugar until stiff peaks form.
7. Once the cakes are cooled, spread a layer of cherry preserves on one cake, then top with whipped cream. Place the second cake on top and repeat with the remaining preserves and whipped cream.
8. Garnish with chocolate shavings and serve.

Churro Cake

Ingredients:

- 1 1/2 cups all-purpose flour
- 1 teaspoon baking powder
- 1/2 teaspoon baking soda
- 1/2 teaspoon cinnamon
- 1/4 teaspoon salt
- 1/2 cup unsalted butter, softened
- 1 cup granulated sugar
- 2 large eggs
- 1 teaspoon vanilla extract
- 1/2 cup sour cream
- 1/4 cup milk

For Cinnamon-Sugar Coating:

- 1/4 cup granulated sugar
- 1 tablespoon ground cinnamon
- 2 tablespoons unsalted butter, melted

Instructions:

1. Preheat the oven to 350°F (175°C). Grease and flour a 9-inch round cake pan.
2. In a bowl, combine the flour, baking powder, baking soda, cinnamon, and salt.
3. In another bowl, beat the butter and sugar until light and fluffy. Add the eggs and vanilla, and mix until smooth.
4. Gradually add the dry ingredients, alternating with sour cream and milk. Mix until combined.
5. Pour the batter into the prepared pan and bake for 25-30 minutes.
6. For the coating, mix the sugar and cinnamon. Once the cake is cooled, brush with melted butter and sprinkle with the cinnamon-sugar mixture.

Chocolate Hazelnut Cake

Ingredients:

- 1 1/2 cups all-purpose flour
- 1 1/2 cups granulated sugar
- 1/2 cup unsweetened cocoa powder
- 1 teaspoon baking soda
- 1/2 teaspoon baking powder
- 1/2 teaspoon salt
- 2 large eggs
- 1 cup buttermilk
- 1/2 cup vegetable oil
- 2 teaspoons vanilla extract
- 1/2 cup chopped hazelnuts

For Hazelnut Frosting:

- 1/2 cup unsalted butter, softened
- 1/4 cup chocolate-hazelnut spread (e.g., Nutella)
- 3 cups powdered sugar
- 2 tablespoons heavy cream
- 1/2 cup chopped hazelnuts for garnish

Instructions:

1. Preheat the oven to 350°F (175°C). Grease and flour two 9-inch round cake pans.
2. In a large bowl, combine the flour, sugar, cocoa powder, baking soda, baking powder, and salt.
3. In another bowl, whisk the eggs, buttermilk, oil, and vanilla. Add to the dry ingredients and mix until smooth.
4. Fold in the chopped hazelnuts.
5. Pour the batter into the pans and bake for 30-35 minutes.
6. For the frosting, beat the butter and chocolate-hazelnut spread together. Gradually add powdered sugar and heavy cream, mixing until smooth.
7. Frost the cooled cakes with hazelnut frosting and garnish with chopped hazelnuts.

Funfetti Cake

Ingredients:

- 2 1/2 cups all-purpose flour
- 1 tablespoon baking powder
- 1/2 teaspoon salt
- 1 cup unsalted butter, softened
- 1 1/2 cups granulated sugar
- 4 large eggs
- 1 teaspoon vanilla extract
- 1 cup milk
- 1/2 cup rainbow sprinkles

For Buttercream Frosting:

- 1/2 cup unsalted butter, softened
- 4 cups powdered sugar
- 2 teaspoons vanilla extract
- 2-3 tablespoons milk
- Rainbow sprinkles for garnish

Instructions:

1. Preheat the oven to 350°F (175°C). Grease and flour two 9-inch round cake pans.
2. In a bowl, combine the flour, baking powder, and salt.
3. In another bowl, beat the butter and sugar until light and fluffy. Add the eggs and vanilla, and mix until smooth.
4. Gradually add the dry ingredients, alternating with the milk, and mix until combined. Fold in the sprinkles.
5. Pour the batter into the pans and bake for 25-30 minutes.
6. For the frosting, beat the butter, powdered sugar, and vanilla until smooth. Add milk to reach the desired consistency.
7. Frost the cooled cakes and garnish with more sprinkles.

Lemon Poppy Seed Cake

Ingredients:

- 2 cups all-purpose flour
- 1 teaspoon baking powder
- 1/2 teaspoon baking soda
- 1/4 teaspoon salt
- 1/2 cup unsalted butter, softened
- 1 1/2 cups granulated sugar
- 3 large eggs
- 1/2 cup sour cream
- 1 tablespoon lemon zest
- 2 tablespoons lemon juice
- 2 tablespoons poppy seeds

For Lemon Glaze:

- 1/2 cup powdered sugar
- 2 tablespoons fresh lemon juice

Instructions:

1. Preheat the oven to 350°F (175°C). Grease and flour a 9-inch round cake pan.
2. In a bowl, mix the flour, baking powder, baking soda, and salt.
3. In another bowl, beat the butter and sugar until creamy. Add the eggs, sour cream, lemon zest, and lemon juice, and mix until smooth.
4. Gradually add the dry ingredients and fold in the poppy seeds.
5. Pour the batter into the pan and bake for 25-30 minutes.
6. For the glaze, whisk together the powdered sugar and lemon juice.
7. Once the cake is cooled, drizzle with the lemon glaze and serve.

Pineapple Upside-Down Cake

Ingredients:

- 1/4 cup unsalted butter
- 1/2 cup brown sugar, packed
- 1 can (20 oz) pineapple slices, drained (reserve juice)
- Maraschino cherries for garnish
- 1 1/2 cups all-purpose flour
- 1 teaspoon baking powder
- 1/2 teaspoon salt
- 1/2 cup unsalted butter, softened
- 1 cup granulated sugar
- 2 large eggs
- 1 teaspoon vanilla extract
- 1/2 cup pineapple juice

Instructions:

1. Preheat the oven to 350°F (175°C). Grease a 9-inch round cake pan.
2. Melt the butter in the pan, then sprinkle with brown sugar. Arrange the pineapple slices in a circle, placing cherries in the center.
3. In a bowl, mix the flour, baking powder, and salt.
4. In another bowl, beat the butter and sugar until fluffy. Add the eggs, vanilla, and pineapple juice, and mix until combined.
5. Gradually add the dry ingredients and mix until smooth.
6. Pour the batter over the pineapple arrangement and bake for 35-40 minutes.
7. Allow the cake to cool for 5 minutes, then invert onto a plate. Serve.

Pistachio Rose Cake

Ingredients:

- 1 1/2 cups all-purpose flour
- 1/2 cup pistachio flour
- 1 1/2 teaspoons baking powder
- 1/4 teaspoon salt
- 1/2 cup unsalted butter, softened
- 1 cup granulated sugar
- 3 large eggs
- 1 teaspoon vanilla extract
- 1/4 cup milk
- 1/4 cup rose water
- 1/2 cup chopped pistachios

For Rose Frosting:

- 1/2 cup unsalted butter, softened
- 3 cups powdered sugar
- 1 teaspoon rose water
- 2-3 tablespoons heavy cream

Instructions:

1. Preheat the oven to 350°F (175°C). Grease and flour a 9-inch round cake pan.
2. In a bowl, mix the flour, pistachio flour, baking powder, and salt.
3. In another bowl, beat the butter and sugar until light and fluffy. Add the eggs and vanilla, and mix until smooth.
4. Gradually add the dry ingredients, alternating with the milk and rose water, and mix until smooth.
5. Fold in the chopped pistachios.
6. Pour the batter into the pan and bake for 25-30 minutes.
7. For the frosting, beat the butter and powdered sugar until smooth. Add rose water and heavy cream to reach the desired consistency.
8. Frost the cooled cake with rose frosting and garnish with chopped pistachios.

Orange and Almond Cake

Ingredients:

- 1 1/2 cups almond meal (or finely ground almonds)
- 1 cup all-purpose flour
- 1 1/2 teaspoons baking powder
- 1/4 teaspoon salt
- 1/2 cup unsalted butter, softened
- 1 cup granulated sugar
- 4 large eggs
- 1 teaspoon vanilla extract
- Zest of 1 large orange
- 1/4 cup fresh orange juice
- Powdered sugar for dusting (optional)

Instructions:

1. Preheat the oven to 350°F (175°C). Grease and line a 9-inch round cake pan.
2. In a bowl, mix the almond meal, flour, baking powder, and salt.
3. In another bowl, beat the butter and sugar until light and fluffy. Add the eggs one at a time, beating well after each addition. Add the vanilla extract, orange zest, and orange juice.
4. Gradually fold in the dry ingredients until smooth.
5. Pour the batter into the prepared pan and bake for 25-30 minutes or until a toothpick comes out clean.
6. Let the cake cool completely, then dust with powdered sugar before serving.

White Chocolate Raspberry Cake

Ingredients:

- 1 1/2 cups all-purpose flour
- 1 teaspoon baking powder
- 1/2 teaspoon baking soda
- 1/4 teaspoon salt
- 1/2 cup unsalted butter, softened
- 1 cup granulated sugar
- 2 large eggs
- 1 teaspoon vanilla extract
- 1/2 cup sour cream
- 1/2 cup white chocolate chips, melted
- 1 cup fresh raspberries

For White Chocolate Frosting:

- 1/2 cup unsalted butter, softened
- 2 cups powdered sugar
- 1/4 cup melted white chocolate
- 1 tablespoon heavy cream
- Fresh raspberries for garnish

Instructions:

1. Preheat the oven to 350°F (175°C). Grease and flour two 9-inch round cake pans.
2. In a bowl, mix the flour, baking powder, baking soda, and salt.
3. In another bowl, beat the butter and sugar until creamy. Add the eggs, one at a time, and beat until smooth. Add the vanilla extract, sour cream, and melted white chocolate.
4. Gradually add the dry ingredients, mixing until just combined. Gently fold in the raspberries.
5. Divide the batter between the two pans and bake for 25-30 minutes.
6. For the frosting, beat the butter and powdered sugar, then add the melted white chocolate and heavy cream until smooth.
7. Frost the cooled cakes with white chocolate frosting and garnish with fresh raspberries.

Cherry Almond Cake

Ingredients:

- 2 cups all-purpose flour
- 1 teaspoon baking powder
- 1/2 teaspoon salt
- 1/2 cup unsalted butter, softened
- 1 cup granulated sugar
- 2 large eggs
- 1 teaspoon almond extract
- 1 cup sour cream
- 1 cup maraschino cherries, chopped and drained

For Almond Frosting:

- 1/2 cup unsalted butter, softened
- 2 cups powdered sugar
- 1 teaspoon almond extract
- 1-2 tablespoons milk
- Maraschino cherries for garnish

Instructions:

1. Preheat the oven to 350°F (175°C). Grease and flour a 9-inch round cake pan.
2. In a bowl, mix the flour, baking powder, and salt.
3. In another bowl, beat the butter and sugar until light and fluffy. Add the eggs one at a time, then mix in the almond extract and sour cream.
4. Gradually fold in the dry ingredients until combined. Stir in the chopped cherries.
5. Pour the batter into the prepared pan and bake for 30-35 minutes.
6. For the frosting, beat the butter and powdered sugar until smooth, then add the almond extract and milk until the desired consistency is reached.
7. Frost the cooled cake with almond frosting and garnish with maraschino cherries.

Hummingbird Cake

Ingredients:

- 2 cups all-purpose flour
- 1 teaspoon baking powder
- 1/2 teaspoon baking soda
- 1/2 teaspoon salt
- 1 teaspoon cinnamon
- 1 1/2 cups granulated sugar
- 3 large eggs
- 1 cup vegetable oil
- 1 teaspoon vanilla extract
- 1 cup crushed pineapple, drained
- 1 cup chopped bananas
- 1/2 cup chopped walnuts
- 1/2 cup shredded coconut

For Cream Cheese Frosting:

- 8 oz cream cheese, softened
- 1/2 cup unsalted butter, softened
- 4 cups powdered sugar
- 1 teaspoon vanilla extract

Instructions:

1. Preheat the oven to 350°F (175°C). Grease and flour two 9-inch round cake pans.
2. In a bowl, mix the flour, baking powder, baking soda, salt, and cinnamon.
3. In another bowl, whisk the sugar, eggs, oil, and vanilla extract. Stir in the pineapple, bananas, walnuts, and coconut.
4. Gradually add the dry ingredients and mix until just combined.
5. Divide the batter between the pans and bake for 30-35 minutes.
6. For the frosting, beat the cream cheese and butter until creamy. Gradually add the powdered sugar and vanilla until smooth.
7. Frost the cooled cakes with cream cheese frosting.

Peach Cobbler Cake

Ingredients:

- 1 1/2 cups all-purpose flour
- 1 teaspoon baking powder
- 1/2 teaspoon baking soda
- 1/4 teaspoon salt
- 1/2 cup unsalted butter, softened
- 1 cup granulated sugar
- 2 large eggs
- 1 teaspoon vanilla extract
- 1/2 cup sour cream
- 1 1/2 cups fresh or canned peaches, diced

For Cinnamon Sugar Topping:

- 1/4 cup granulated sugar
- 1 teaspoon cinnamon

Instructions:

1. Preheat the oven to 350°F (175°C). Grease and flour a 9-inch square baking dish.
2. In a bowl, mix the flour, baking powder, baking soda, and salt.
3. In another bowl, beat the butter and sugar until creamy. Add the eggs and vanilla extract, mixing well.
4. Add the sour cream and dry ingredients, mixing until smooth. Fold in the diced peaches.
5. Pour the batter into the prepared baking dish.
6. In a small bowl, mix the sugar and cinnamon, and sprinkle it over the top of the cake.
7. Bake for 35-40 minutes or until a toothpick comes out clean.

Peanut Butter Chocolate Cake

Ingredients:

- 1 1/2 cups all-purpose flour
- 1/2 cup unsweetened cocoa powder
- 1 teaspoon baking soda
- 1/2 teaspoon salt
- 1/2 cup unsalted butter, softened
- 1 cup granulated sugar
- 2 large eggs
- 1 teaspoon vanilla extract
- 1/2 cup milk
- 1/2 cup peanut butter

For Peanut Butter Frosting:

- 1/2 cup unsalted butter, softened
- 1/2 cup peanut butter
- 3 cups powdered sugar
- 2 tablespoons milk
- 1/2 teaspoon vanilla extract

Instructions:

1. Preheat the oven to 350°F (175°C). Grease and flour two 9-inch round cake pans.
2. In a bowl, mix the flour, cocoa powder, baking soda, and salt.
3. In another bowl, beat the butter and sugar until creamy. Add the eggs one at a time, followed by the vanilla extract.
4. Mix in the milk and peanut butter until smooth.
5. Gradually add the dry ingredients and mix until combined.
6. Pour the batter into the pans and bake for 25-30 minutes.
7. For the frosting, beat the butter and peanut butter together. Gradually add the powdered sugar, milk, and vanilla until smooth.
8. Frost the cooled cakes with peanut butter frosting.

Tres Leches Cake

Ingredients:

- 1 1/2 cups all-purpose flour
- 1 1/2 teaspoons baking powder
- 1/4 teaspoon salt
- 1/2 cup unsalted butter, softened
- 1 cup granulated sugar
- 5 large eggs
- 1 teaspoon vanilla extract
- 1 cup whole milk

For Tres Leches Soak:

- 1/2 cup heavy cream
- 1/2 cup evaporated milk
- 1/2 cup sweetened condensed milk

For Whipped Cream Topping:

- 1 cup heavy cream
- 1/4 cup powdered sugar
- 1 teaspoon vanilla extract

Instructions:

1. Preheat the oven to 350°F (175°C). Grease and flour a 9-inch round cake pan.
2. In a bowl, mix the flour, baking powder, and salt.
3. In another bowl, beat the butter and sugar until light and fluffy. Add the eggs one at a time, then add the vanilla.
4. Gradually add the dry ingredients, alternating with the milk, until smooth.
5. Pour the batter into the prepared pan and bake for 25-30 minutes.
6. Once baked, combine the heavy cream, evaporated milk, and condensed milk for the soak.
7. Poke holes in the cake with a fork and pour the milk mixture over the cake, letting it soak in.
8. For the topping, whip the heavy cream, powdered sugar, and vanilla until soft peaks form. Spread over the cake before serving.

Poppy Seed Cake

Ingredients:

- 1 1/2 cups all-purpose flour
- 1 teaspoon baking powder
- 1/4 teaspoon salt
- 1/2 cup unsalted butter, softened
- 1 cup granulated sugar
- 3 large eggs
- 1 teaspoon vanilla extract
- 1 tablespoon poppy seeds
- 1/2 cup sour cream

Instructions:

1. Preheat the oven to 350°F (175°C). Grease and flour a 9-inch round cake pan.
2. In a bowl, mix the flour, baking powder, and salt.
3. In another bowl, beat the butter and sugar until fluffy. Add the eggs and vanilla extract, and beat until smooth.
4. Gradually add the dry ingredients, mixing until smooth. Fold in the poppy seeds.
5. Pour the batter into the prepared pan and bake for 25-30 minutes.
6. Cool the cake before serving.

Caramelized Banana Cake

Ingredients:

- 1 1/2 cups all-purpose flour
- 1 teaspoon baking soda
- 1/2 teaspoon salt
- 1/2 cup unsalted butter, softened
- 1 cup brown sugar
- 2 large eggs
- 2 ripe bananas, mashed
- 1 teaspoon vanilla extract
- 1/2 cup buttermilk

For Caramelized Bananas:

- 2 ripe bananas, sliced
- 1/4 cup brown sugar
- 1 tablespoon butter

Instructions:

1. Preheat the oven to 350°F (175°C). Grease and flour a 9-inch round cake pan.
2. In a bowl, mix the flour, baking soda, and salt.
3. In another bowl, beat the butter and brown sugar until creamy. Add the eggs, mashed bananas, and vanilla extract.
4. Gradually add the dry ingredients, mixing until smooth. Add the buttermilk and mix well.
5. For the caramelized bananas, melt the butter in a pan, then add the sliced bananas and brown sugar. Cook until the bananas are softened and caramelized.
6. Pour the batter into the prepared pan, then spoon the caramelized bananas over the top.
7. Bake for 30-35 minutes or until a toothpick comes out clean. Let cool before serving.

German Chocolate Cake

Ingredients:

- 1 1/2 cups all-purpose flour
- 1 teaspoon baking powder
- 1/2 teaspoon baking soda
- 1/4 teaspoon salt
- 1/2 cup unsweetened cocoa powder
- 1 cup granulated sugar
- 1/2 cup unsalted butter, softened
- 2 large eggs
- 1 teaspoon vanilla extract
- 1 cup buttermilk
- 1 cup boiling water
- 1/2 cup shredded coconut
- 1/2 cup chopped pecans

For Frosting:

- 1/2 cup unsalted butter
- 1 cup evaporated milk
- 1 cup granulated sugar
- 3 large egg yolks
- 1 teaspoon vanilla extract
- 1 1/2 cups shredded coconut
- 1/2 cup chopped pecans

Instructions:

1. Preheat the oven to 350°F (175°C). Grease and flour two 9-inch round cake pans.
2. In a bowl, mix the flour, baking powder, baking soda, salt, and cocoa powder.
3. In another bowl, beat the butter and sugar until creamy. Add the eggs, one at a time, followed by the vanilla extract.
4. Gradually add the dry ingredients, alternating with the buttermilk, until combined. Stir in the boiling water (the batter will be thin).
5. Pour the batter into the pans and bake for 25-30 minutes or until a toothpick comes out clean.

6. For the frosting, combine butter, evaporated milk, sugar, and egg yolks in a saucepan. Cook over medium heat, whisking constantly until thickened. Remove from heat and stir in vanilla extract, coconut, and pecans.
7. Frost the cooled cakes with the coconut-pecan frosting.

Mocha Hazelnut Cake

Ingredients:

- 1 1/2 cups all-purpose flour
- 1/2 cup unsweetened cocoa powder
- 1 teaspoon baking powder
- 1/2 teaspoon baking soda
- 1/4 teaspoon salt
- 1 cup granulated sugar
- 1/2 cup unsalted butter, softened
- 2 large eggs
- 1 teaspoon vanilla extract
- 1/2 cup strong brewed coffee
- 1/2 cup hazelnut meal or ground hazelnuts
- 1/2 cup sour cream

For Mocha Frosting:

- 1/2 cup unsalted butter, softened
- 1 cup powdered sugar
- 1 tablespoon cocoa powder
- 2 tablespoons strong brewed coffee
- 1/2 cup finely ground hazelnuts

Instructions:

1. Preheat the oven to 350°F (175°C). Grease and flour two 9-inch round cake pans.
2. In a bowl, mix the flour, cocoa powder, baking powder, baking soda, and salt.
3. In another bowl, beat the butter and sugar until light and fluffy. Add the eggs, one at a time, then add the vanilla extract.
4. Gradually add the dry ingredients, alternating with the coffee and sour cream, until smooth.
5. Fold in the hazelnut meal.
6. Pour the batter into the pans and bake for 25-30 minutes.
7. For the frosting, beat the butter, powdered sugar, cocoa powder, and coffee until smooth. Frost the cooled cakes and sprinkle with ground hazelnuts.

Vanilla Bean Pound Cake

Ingredients:

- 2 cups all-purpose flour
- 1 teaspoon baking powder
- 1/4 teaspoon salt
- 1 cup unsalted butter, softened
- 2 cups granulated sugar
- 4 large eggs
- 1 tablespoon vanilla bean paste or vanilla extract
- 1 cup sour cream

Instructions:

1. Preheat the oven to 350°F (175°C). Grease and flour a 9x5-inch loaf pan.
2. In a bowl, mix the flour, baking powder, and salt.
3. In another bowl, beat the butter and sugar until fluffy. Add the eggs, one at a time, mixing well after each addition. Add the vanilla.
4. Gradually add the dry ingredients, alternating with the sour cream, until smooth.
5. Pour the batter into the prepared pan and bake for 55-60 minutes or until a toothpick comes out clean.
6. Let the cake cool completely before slicing.

Coconut Pineapple Cake

Ingredients:

- 1 1/2 cups all-purpose flour
- 1 teaspoon baking powder
- 1/2 teaspoon baking soda
- 1/4 teaspoon salt
- 1 cup unsalted butter, softened
- 1 1/2 cups granulated sugar
- 2 large eggs
- 1 teaspoon vanilla extract
- 1 cup crushed pineapple, drained
- 1/2 cup shredded coconut
- 1/2 cup buttermilk

For Frosting:

- 8 oz cream cheese, softened
- 1/4 cup unsalted butter, softened
- 2 cups powdered sugar
- 1 teaspoon vanilla extract
- 1/2 cup shredded coconut

Instructions:

1. Preheat the oven to 350°F (175°C). Grease and flour two 9-inch round cake pans.
2. In a bowl, mix the flour, baking powder, baking soda, and salt.
3. In another bowl, beat the butter and sugar until light and fluffy. Add the eggs, one at a time, then add the vanilla extract.
4. Gradually add the dry ingredients, alternating with the buttermilk, until smooth. Stir in the pineapple and coconut.
5. Pour the batter into the pans and bake for 25-30 minutes.
6. For the frosting, beat the cream cheese and butter until smooth. Gradually add the powdered sugar and vanilla extract. Frost the cooled cakes and top with shredded coconut.

Pumpkin Spice Cake

Ingredients:

- 2 cups all-purpose flour
- 1 teaspoon baking powder
- 1 teaspoon baking soda
- 1/2 teaspoon salt
- 1 tablespoon ground cinnamon
- 1/2 teaspoon ground nutmeg
- 1/4 teaspoon ground ginger
- 1/4 teaspoon ground cloves
- 1 cup granulated sugar
- 1/2 cup unsalted butter, softened
- 2 large eggs
- 1 cup canned pumpkin puree
- 1 teaspoon vanilla extract

For Cream Cheese Frosting:

- 8 oz cream cheese, softened
- 1/4 cup unsalted butter, softened
- 2 cups powdered sugar
- 1 teaspoon vanilla extract

Instructions:

1. Preheat the oven to 350°F (175°C). Grease and flour two 9-inch round cake pans.
2. In a bowl, mix the flour, baking powder, baking soda, salt, cinnamon, nutmeg, ginger, and cloves.
3. In another bowl, beat the sugar and butter until creamy. Add the eggs, one at a time, then add the pumpkin puree and vanilla extract.
4. Gradually add the dry ingredients and mix until combined.
5. Pour the batter into the pans and bake for 25-30 minutes.
6. For the frosting, beat the cream cheese and butter until creamy. Gradually add the powdered sugar and vanilla extract.
7. Frost the cooled cakes with cream cheese frosting.

Black Sesame Cake

Ingredients:

- 1 1/2 cups all-purpose flour
- 1/2 teaspoon baking powder
- 1/4 teaspoon salt
- 1/2 cup unsalted butter, softened
- 3/4 cup granulated sugar
- 2 large eggs
- 1/2 cup black sesame paste
- 1/4 cup milk
- 1 teaspoon vanilla extract

For Frosting:

- 1/2 cup unsalted butter, softened
- 2 cups powdered sugar
- 1/4 cup black sesame paste
- 1 tablespoon milk

Instructions:

1. Preheat the oven to 350°F (175°C). Grease and flour two 9-inch round cake pans.
2. In a bowl, mix the flour, baking powder, and salt.
3. In another bowl, beat the butter and sugar until creamy. Add the eggs, one at a time, then add the black sesame paste, milk, and vanilla extract.
4. Gradually add the dry ingredients and mix until smooth.
5. Pour the batter into the pans and bake for 25-30 minutes.
6. For the frosting, beat the butter and powdered sugar until smooth. Add the black sesame paste and milk, mixing until creamy.
7. Frost the cooled cakes with black sesame frosting.

Chocolate Mousse Cake

Ingredients:

- 1 1/2 cups all-purpose flour
- 1/2 cup unsweetened cocoa powder
- 1 teaspoon baking powder
- 1/2 teaspoon baking soda
- 1/4 teaspoon salt
- 1 cup granulated sugar
- 1/2 cup unsalted butter, softened
- 2 large eggs
- 1 teaspoon vanilla extract
- 1 cup buttermilk

For Mousse Filling:

- 8 oz semi-sweet chocolate, chopped
- 1 cup heavy cream
- 1 teaspoon vanilla extract

For Ganache:

- 4 oz semi-sweet chocolate, chopped
- 1/4 cup heavy cream

Instructions:

1. Preheat the oven to 350°F (175°C). Grease and flour two 9-inch round cake pans.
2. In a bowl, mix the flour, cocoa powder, baking powder, baking soda, and salt.
3. In another bowl, beat the butter and sugar until fluffy. Add the eggs and vanilla extract.
4. Gradually add the dry ingredients, alternating with the buttermilk, until smooth.
5. Pour the batter into the pans and bake for 25-30 minutes.
6. For the mousse, melt the chocolate in a heatproof bowl. Whisk the heavy cream until soft peaks form, then fold it into the melted chocolate with vanilla extract.
7. For the ganache, heat the cream in a saucepan and pour over the chopped chocolate. Stir until smooth.
8. Once the cakes have cooled, spread a layer of mousse on top of one cake, then place the second cake on top. Pour the ganache over the top.

Matcha Green Tea Cake

Ingredients:

- 1 1/2 cups all-purpose flour
- 1 teaspoon baking powder
- 1/4 teaspoon salt
- 1/4 cup unsalted butter, softened
- 1 cup granulated sugar
- 3 large eggs
- 1 tablespoon matcha powder
- 1/2 cup milk
- 1 teaspoon vanilla extract

For Frosting:

- 8 oz cream cheese, softened
- 1/4 cup unsalted butter, softened
- 2 cups powdered sugar
- 1 tablespoon matcha powder

Instructions:

1. Preheat the oven to 350°F (175°C). Grease and flour two 9-inch round cake pans.
2. In a bowl, mix the flour, baking powder, and salt.
3. In another bowl, beat the butter and sugar until light and fluffy. Add the eggs, one at a time, then add the matcha powder, milk, and vanilla extract.
4. Gradually add the dry ingredients and mix until smooth.
5. Pour the batter into the pans and bake for 25-30 minutes.
6. For the frosting, beat the cream cheese and butter until smooth. Gradually add the powdered sugar and matcha powder.
7. Frost the cooled cakes with matcha cream cheese frosting.

S'mores Cake

Ingredients:

- 1 1/2 cups all-purpose flour
- 1/2 teaspoon baking powder
- 1/4 teaspoon salt
- 1/2 cup unsweetened cocoa powder
- 1 cup granulated sugar
- 1/2 cup unsalted butter, softened
- 2 large eggs
- 1 teaspoon vanilla extract
- 1 cup milk
- 1/2 cup graham cracker crumbs

For Marshmallow Frosting:

- 1 cup marshmallow fluff
- 1/2 cup unsalted butter, softened
- 2 cups powdered sugar

For Chocolate Ganache:

- 4 oz semi-sweet chocolate, chopped
- 1/4 cup heavy cream

Instructions:

1. Preheat the oven to 350°F (175°C). Grease and flour two 9-inch round cake pans.
2. In a bowl, mix the flour, baking powder, salt, and cocoa powder.
3. In another bowl, beat the butter and sugar until fluffy. Add the eggs and vanilla extract.
4. Gradually add the dry ingredients, alternating with the milk, until smooth.
5. Fold in the graham cracker crumbs.
6. Pour the batter into the pans and bake for 25-30 minutes.
7. For the frosting, beat the marshmallow fluff, butter, and powdered sugar until smooth.
8. For the ganache, heat the cream and pour over the chopped chocolate, stirring until smooth.
9. Frost the cooled cakes with marshmallow frosting, then drizzle with chocolate ganache.

Maple Pecan Cake

Ingredients:

- 1 1/2 cups all-purpose flour
- 1 teaspoon baking powder
- 1/2 teaspoon baking soda
- 1/4 teaspoon salt
- 1/2 cup unsalted butter, softened
- 1 cup granulated sugar
- 2 large eggs
- 1/2 cup pure maple syrup
- 1 teaspoon vanilla extract
- 1/2 cup milk
- 1/2 cup chopped pecans, toasted

For Maple Frosting:

- 1/2 cup unsalted butter, softened
- 2 cups powdered sugar
- 1/4 cup pure maple syrup
- 1 teaspoon vanilla extract

Instructions:

1. Preheat the oven to 350°F (175°C). Grease and flour two 9-inch round cake pans.
2. In a bowl, mix the flour, baking powder, baking soda, and salt.
3. In another bowl, beat the butter and sugar until creamy. Add the eggs, one at a time, then add the maple syrup and vanilla extract.
4. Gradually add the dry ingredients, alternating with the milk, until smooth.
5. Fold in the toasted pecans.
6. Pour the batter into the pans and bake for 25-30 minutes.
7. For the frosting, beat the butter, powdered sugar, maple syrup, and vanilla extract until smooth.
8. Frost the cooled cakes with the maple frosting.

Lime Coconut Cake

Ingredients:

- 1 1/2 cups all-purpose flour
- 1 teaspoon baking powder
- 1/2 teaspoon baking soda
- 1/4 teaspoon salt
- 1/2 cup unsalted butter, softened
- 1 cup granulated sugar
- 2 large eggs
- 1/4 cup fresh lime juice
- 1/2 cup shredded coconut
- 1/2 cup milk
- Zest of 2 limes

For Coconut Lime Frosting:

- 8 oz cream cheese, softened
- 1/4 cup unsalted butter, softened
- 2 cups powdered sugar
- 1 teaspoon vanilla extract
- 1/2 cup shredded coconut, toasted

Instructions:

1. Preheat the oven to 350°F (175°C). Grease and flour two 9-inch round cake pans.
2. In a bowl, mix the flour, baking powder, baking soda, and salt.
3. In another bowl, beat the butter and sugar until fluffy. Add the eggs, one at a time, then add the lime juice, lime zest, and coconut.
4. Gradually add the dry ingredients, alternating with the milk, until smooth.
5. Pour the batter into the pans and bake for 25-30 minutes.
6. For the frosting, beat the cream cheese and butter until smooth. Gradually add the powdered sugar and vanilla extract.
7. Frost the cooled cakes with the coconut lime frosting and top with toasted coconut.

Vanilla Chiffon Cake

Ingredients:

- 1 3/4 cups all-purpose flour
- 1 teaspoon baking powder
- 1/2 teaspoon baking soda
- 1/4 teaspoon salt
- 1/2 cup vegetable oil
- 5 large eggs, separated
- 1 cup granulated sugar
- 1 teaspoon vanilla extract
- 3/4 cup water
- 1/2 teaspoon cream of tartar

For Whipped Cream Frosting:

- 2 cups heavy cream
- 1/4 cup powdered sugar
- 1 teaspoon vanilla extract

Instructions:

1. Preheat the oven to 325°F (165°C). Grease and flour a 10-inch tube pan.
2. In a bowl, mix the flour, baking powder, baking soda, and salt.
3. In another bowl, whisk the egg yolks, oil, sugar, vanilla extract, and water until smooth.
4. Gradually add the dry ingredients to the wet ingredients and mix until combined.
5. In a separate bowl, beat the egg whites with cream of tartar until stiff peaks form.
6. Gently fold the egg whites into the batter until just combined.
7. Pour the batter into the pan and bake for 55-60 minutes.
8. For the frosting, whip the heavy cream, powdered sugar, and vanilla extract until stiff peaks form.
9. Frost the cooled cake with whipped cream.

Brown Sugar Cinnamon Cake

Ingredients:

- 1 1/2 cups all-purpose flour
- 1 teaspoon baking powder
- 1/2 teaspoon baking soda
- 1/4 teaspoon salt
- 1 tablespoon ground cinnamon
- 1 cup unsalted butter, softened
- 1 cup brown sugar, packed
- 2 large eggs
- 1 teaspoon vanilla extract
- 1/2 cup milk

For Cinnamon Brown Sugar Frosting:

- 1/2 cup unsalted butter, softened
- 2 cups powdered sugar
- 1 tablespoon ground cinnamon
- 1 tablespoon milk

Instructions:

1. Preheat the oven to 350°F (175°C). Grease and flour two 9-inch round cake pans.
2. In a bowl, mix the flour, baking powder, baking soda, salt, and cinnamon.
3. In another bowl, beat the butter and brown sugar until creamy. Add the eggs, one at a time, then add the vanilla extract.
4. Gradually add the dry ingredients, alternating with the milk, until smooth.
5. Pour the batter into the pans and bake for 25-30 minutes.
6. For the frosting, beat the butter, powdered sugar, cinnamon, and milk until smooth.
7. Frost the cooled cakes with the cinnamon brown sugar frosting.

Apricot Almond Cake

Ingredients:

- 1 1/2 cups all-purpose flour
- 1 teaspoon baking powder
- 1/4 teaspoon salt
- 1/2 cup unsalted butter, softened
- 1 cup granulated sugar
- 3 large eggs
- 1 teaspoon vanilla extract
- 1/4 cup apricot jam
- 1/2 cup ground almonds
- 1/2 cup milk

For Almond Cream Frosting:

- 8 oz cream cheese, softened
- 1/4 cup unsalted butter, softened
- 1 cup powdered sugar
- 1/4 cup ground almonds
- 1 teaspoon vanilla extract

Instructions:

1. Preheat the oven to 350°F (175°C). Grease and flour two 9-inch round cake pans.
2. In a bowl, mix the flour, baking powder, and salt.
3. In another bowl, beat the butter and sugar until fluffy. Add the eggs, one at a time, followed by the vanilla extract and apricot jam.
4. Gradually add the dry ingredients, alternating with the ground almonds and milk, until smooth.
5. Pour the batter into the pans and bake for 25-30 minutes.
6. For the frosting, beat the cream cheese, butter, powdered sugar, ground almonds, and vanilla extract until smooth.
7. Frost the cooled cakes with almond cream frosting.

Spiced Apple Cake

Ingredients:

- 1 1/2 cups all-purpose flour
- 1 teaspoon baking powder
- 1 teaspoon ground cinnamon
- 1/4 teaspoon ground nutmeg
- 1/4 teaspoon ground cloves
- 1/4 teaspoon salt
- 1/2 cup unsalted butter, softened
- 1 cup granulated sugar
- 2 large eggs
- 1 teaspoon vanilla extract
- 1 cup finely grated apple (peeled)
- 1/2 cup milk

For Cinnamon Cream Cheese Frosting:

- 8 oz cream cheese, softened
- 1/4 cup unsalted butter, softened
- 2 cups powdered sugar
- 1 teaspoon cinnamon

Instructions:

1. Preheat the oven to 350°F (175°C). Grease and flour two 9-inch round cake pans.
2. In a bowl, mix the flour, baking powder, cinnamon, nutmeg, cloves, and salt.
3. In another bowl, beat the butter and sugar until fluffy. Add the eggs, one at a time, then add the vanilla extract and grated apple.
4. Gradually add the dry ingredients, alternating with the milk, until smooth.
5. Pour the batter into the pans and bake for 25-30 minutes.
6. For the frosting, beat the cream cheese, butter, powdered sugar, and cinnamon until smooth.
7. Frost the cooled cakes with cinnamon cream cheese frosting.

Meringue Layer Cake

Ingredients:

- 1 1/2 cups all-purpose flour
- 1 teaspoon baking powder
- 1/4 teaspoon salt
- 1 cup unsalted butter, softened
- 1 cup granulated sugar
- 4 large eggs, separated
- 1 teaspoon vanilla extract
- 1/2 cup milk
- 1 cup whipped egg whites (from the separated egg whites)

For Meringue Layers:

- 4 large egg whites
- 1 cup granulated sugar
- 1 teaspoon vanilla extract

For Frosting:

- 1 cup heavy cream
- 1/4 cup powdered sugar
- 1 teaspoon vanilla extract

Instructions:

1. Preheat the oven to 350°F (175°C). Grease and flour two 9-inch round cake pans.
2. In a bowl, mix the flour, baking powder, and salt.
3. In another bowl, beat the butter and sugar until creamy. Add the egg yolks, one at a time, followed by vanilla extract and milk.
4. Gently fold in the whipped egg whites.
5. For the meringue, beat the egg whites and sugar until stiff peaks form, then add vanilla extract.
6. Layer the meringue on top of the cake layers, then bake for 25-30 minutes.
7. For the frosting, whip the heavy cream, powdered sugar, and vanilla extract until stiff peaks form.
8. Frost the cooled cakes with whipped cream.

Baked Alaska Cake

Ingredients:

- 1 1/2 cups all-purpose flour
- 1 teaspoon baking powder
- 1/4 teaspoon salt
- 1/2 cup unsalted butter, softened
- 1 cup granulated sugar
- 4 large eggs
- 1 teaspoon vanilla extract
- 1/2 cup milk

For Ice Cream:

- 1 quart vanilla ice cream
- 1/4 cup rum or fruit juice

For Meringue:

- 4 large egg whites
- 1/2 cup granulated sugar
- 1 teaspoon vanilla extract

Instructions:

1. Preheat the oven to 350°F (175°C). Grease and flour two 9-inch round cake pans.
2. In a bowl, mix the flour, baking powder, and salt.
3. In another bowl, beat the butter and sugar until fluffy. Add the eggs, one at a time, and then add the vanilla extract.
4. Gradually add the dry ingredients, alternating with the milk, until smooth.
5. Bake for 25-30 minutes, then let the cakes cool.
6. Soften the vanilla ice cream and spread it over one cake layer. Place the second cake on top and freeze for 2 hours.
7. For the meringue, beat the egg whites and sugar until stiff peaks form, then add the vanilla extract.
8. Spread the meringue over the cake and ice cream, then bake at 400°F for 5-7 minutes until golden brown.

Lemon Raspberry Meringue Cake

Ingredients:

- 1 1/2 cups all-purpose flour
- 1 teaspoon baking powder
- 1/4 teaspoon salt
- 1/2 cup unsalted butter, softened
- 1 cup granulated sugar
- 3 large eggs
- 1 teaspoon vanilla extract
- Zest of 1 lemon
- 1/2 cup milk
- 1 cup raspberries

For Meringue:

- 4 large egg whites
- 1 cup granulated sugar
- 1 teaspoon vanilla extract

For Frosting:

- 1 cup heavy cream
- 1/4 cup powdered sugar
- 1 teaspoon vanilla extract

Instructions:

1. Preheat the oven to 350°F (175°C). Grease and flour two 9-inch round cake pans.
2. In a bowl, mix the flour, baking powder, and salt.
3. In another bowl, beat the butter and sugar until fluffy. Add the eggs, one at a time, then add the vanilla extract and lemon zest.
4. Gradually add the dry ingredients, alternating with the milk, until smooth.
5. Gently fold in the raspberries.
6. Bake the cake for 25-30 minutes, then cool.
7. For the meringue, beat the egg whites and sugar until stiff peaks form, then add the vanilla extract.
8. Frost the cooled cake with whipped cream and top with meringue.

Key Lime Cake

Ingredients:

- 1 1/2 cups all-purpose flour
- 1 teaspoon baking powder
- 1/2 teaspoon baking soda
- 1/4 teaspoon salt
- 1/2 cup unsalted butter, softened
- 1 cup granulated sugar
- 2 large eggs
- Zest of 2 key limes
- 1/4 cup fresh key lime juice
- 1/2 cup buttermilk

For Lime Cream Cheese Frosting:

- 8 oz cream cheese, softened
- 1/4 cup unsalted butter, softened
- 2 cups powdered sugar
- 2 tablespoons fresh key lime juice
- Zest of 1 key lime

Instructions:

1. Preheat the oven to 350°F (175°C). Grease and flour two 9-inch round cake pans.
2. In a bowl, mix the flour, baking powder, baking soda, and salt.
3. In another bowl, beat the butter and sugar until fluffy. Add the eggs, one at a time, then add the lime zest and juice.
4. Gradually add the dry ingredients, alternating with the buttermilk, until smooth.
5. Pour the batter into the pans and bake for 25-30 minutes, or until a toothpick comes out clean.
6. For the frosting, beat the cream cheese and butter until creamy. Add the powdered sugar, lime juice, and zest, and mix until smooth.
7. Frost the cooled cakes with lime cream cheese frosting.

Lavender Honey Cake

Ingredients:

- 1 1/2 cups all-purpose flour
- 1 teaspoon baking powder
- 1/2 teaspoon baking soda
- 1/4 teaspoon salt
- 1/2 cup unsalted butter, softened
- 3/4 cup honey
- 2 large eggs
- 1 teaspoon vanilla extract
- 1/4 cup whole milk
- 1 tablespoon dried lavender flowers (or 1 teaspoon lavender extract)

For Honey Lavender Buttercream:

- 1/2 cup unsalted butter, softened
- 2 cups powdered sugar
- 2 tablespoons honey
- 1 teaspoon lavender extract (or a few drops of lavender essential oil)

Instructions:

1. Preheat the oven to 350°F (175°C). Grease and flour two 9-inch round cake pans.
2. In a bowl, mix the flour, baking powder, baking soda, and salt.
3. In another bowl, beat the butter and honey until smooth. Add the eggs, one at a time, then add the vanilla extract.
4. Gradually add the dry ingredients, alternating with the milk, until smooth. Add the lavender flowers or extract and mix well.
5. Pour the batter into the pans and bake for 25-30 minutes.
6. For the buttercream, beat the butter until smooth, then add the powdered sugar, honey, and lavender extract. Mix until creamy.
7. Frost the cooled cakes with the honey lavender buttercream.

Chococherry Cake

Ingredients:

- 1 1/2 cups all-purpose flour
- 1/2 cup cocoa powder
- 1 teaspoon baking powder
- 1/2 teaspoon baking soda
- 1/4 teaspoon salt
- 1/2 cup unsalted butter, softened
- 1 cup granulated sugar
- 2 large eggs
- 1 teaspoon vanilla extract
- 1 cup sour cream
- 1/2 cup maraschino cherries, chopped, with juice

For Chocolate Cherry Frosting:

- 8 oz cream cheese, softened
- 1/2 cup unsalted butter, softened
- 2 cups powdered sugar
- 1/4 cup cocoa powder
- 2 tablespoons maraschino cherry juice

Instructions:

1. Preheat the oven to 350°F (175°C). Grease and flour two 9-inch round cake pans.
2. In a bowl, mix the flour, cocoa powder, baking powder, baking soda, and salt.
3. In another bowl, beat the butter and sugar until fluffy. Add the eggs, one at a time, followed by the vanilla extract.
4. Gradually add the dry ingredients, alternating with the sour cream, until smooth. Fold in the chopped cherries and juice.
5. Pour the batter into the pans and bake for 25-30 minutes.
6. For the frosting, beat the cream cheese and butter until smooth. Add the powdered sugar, cocoa powder, and cherry juice and mix until creamy.
7. Frost the cooled cakes with the chocolate cherry frosting.

Apple Cinnamon Streusel Cake

Ingredients:

- 1 1/2 cups all-purpose flour
- 1 teaspoon baking powder
- 1/2 teaspoon baking soda
- 1/4 teaspoon salt
- 1 teaspoon ground cinnamon
- 1/2 cup unsalted butter, softened
- 3/4 cup granulated sugar
- 2 large eggs
- 1 teaspoon vanilla extract
- 1 cup finely chopped apples (peeled)
- 1/2 cup sour cream

For Streusel Topping:

- 1/2 cup all-purpose flour
- 1/4 cup brown sugar
- 1 teaspoon ground cinnamon
- 1/4 cup unsalted butter, softened

For Cinnamon Glaze:

- 1/2 cup powdered sugar
- 1 tablespoon milk
- 1/2 teaspoon ground cinnamon

Instructions:

1. Preheat the oven to 350°F (175°C). Grease and flour a 9-inch round cake pan.
2. In a bowl, mix the flour, baking powder, baking soda, salt, and cinnamon.
3. In another bowl, beat the butter and sugar until fluffy. Add the eggs, one at a time, followed by the vanilla extract.
4. Gradually add the dry ingredients, alternating with the sour cream, until smooth. Fold in the chopped apples.
5. For the streusel topping, mix the flour, brown sugar, cinnamon, and butter until crumbly.
6. Pour the batter into the pan and sprinkle the streusel topping on top.
7. Bake for 30-35 minutes, or until a toothpick comes out clean.

8. For the glaze, whisk together the powdered sugar, milk, and cinnamon until smooth. Drizzle over the cooled cake.

White Chocolate Mint Cake

Ingredients:

- 1 1/2 cups all-purpose flour
- 1 teaspoon baking powder
- 1/4 teaspoon salt
- 1/2 cup unsalted butter, softened
- 1 cup granulated sugar
- 3 large eggs
- 1 teaspoon vanilla extract
- 1/2 teaspoon peppermint extract
- 1/2 cup whole milk
- 1/2 cup white chocolate chips, melted

For White Chocolate Mint Buttercream:

- 1/2 cup unsalted butter, softened
- 2 cups powdered sugar
- 1/2 teaspoon peppermint extract
- 2 tablespoons white chocolate chips, melted
- 1-2 tablespoons milk (for desired consistency)

Instructions:

1. Preheat the oven to 350°F (175°C). Grease and flour two 9-inch round cake pans.
2. In a bowl, mix the flour, baking powder, and salt.
3. In another bowl, beat the butter and sugar until fluffy. Add the eggs, one at a time, followed by the vanilla and peppermint extracts.
4. Gradually add the dry ingredients, alternating with the milk, until smooth. Fold in the melted white chocolate.
5. Pour the batter into the pans and bake for 25-30 minutes.
6. For the buttercream, beat the butter until smooth. Add the powdered sugar, peppermint extract, and melted white chocolate. Gradually add milk to reach desired consistency.
7. Frost the cooled cakes with white chocolate mint buttercream.